Free Range Angels

Poems by

Thomas Zimmerman

ISBN: 978-93-6354-475-8

First Edition: 2025
Rs. 200/-

Cyberwit.net
HIG 45 Kaushambi Kunj, Kalindipuram
Allahabad - 211011 (U.P.) India
http://www.cyberwit.net
Tel: +(91) 9415091004
E-mail: info@cyberwit.net

Printed at Repro India Limited.

Acknowledgments

My thanks to the editors of the following publications, where earlier versions of the poems in this book first appeared:

Ablanatha, Active Muse, Amaryllis, Blood + Honey, Brief Wilderness, Cold Signal, dadakuku, DarkWinter Magazine, Dog Throat Journal, Earth Mother/Mother Earth, Exquisite Death, Feed the Holy, Full House, Kinpaurak, A Light in the Darkness, Lowlife Lit, Magpie, Masked & Unmasked, Northwest Indiana Literary Journal, Orenaug Mountain Poetry Journal, The Paradox, Partially Shy, Periwinkle Pelican, Pulsebeat Poetry Journal, Punk Monk Magazine, Revolutionary Love, Soul Poetry, Spare Parts, Summer Visions, To Write a Refuge, TrashLight, Trouvaille Review, Yellow Mama.

Earlier versions of the poems in section III of this book first appeared in my chapbooks *Mr Cinnamon* and *Yet Another Life*, both from Zetataurus Press.

Cover art by the author.

Author photograph by Ann Zimmerman.

Contents

I. Free

Appendix

I.
Free

absinthe carpet

so Rimbaud's bellowing the country band
that's backing him lays down an absinthe carpet
sound   that is to say i'm listening
to Dylan   //   grad school memories rise bright
& glistening evaporate they could
be blessèd souls ascending heaven   really
they're just bubbles in my beer & i
remember one guy so damned smart his only
answer in the seminars was laughter
//   i'm a middling muddler   beancount angel
scolds *you idiot stop writing poems*
i have my moments though   imagining
ambivalent horizons   painted drywall
i with wit & luck could kick clean through

bedtime story (ii)

dog stretched out snoring on an old bedsheet
it could be me   you say that we two sound
& sometimes smell the same   //   train whistle blows
its lonesome trope from way downtown   such voices
trouble us   oh where are goods & people
going   why are we stuck here in midwest
middle age with bills & pulp of commerce
wrinkled without wisdom comical
when naked   //   i say love of poems has saved
my life   the bedside table groans with books
they crowd each nook some even casting shadow
onto shadow in the turned off oven
i won't burn them swear   all screaming i'm
alive   catharsis yes let's go to bed

Callie's eternal spring

an April night the Christmas lights still up
oh it's alright all time is one it's always
now   sweet mantras for bohemians
god love 'em   //   rain & sun & greening up
your precious hormones catching fire & even
though the poet you're in lust with says
he doesn't give a damn about your dreams
you don't believe him   //   dark red blossoms on
the bush out front & gauze balls on the neighbors'
tree   the beer you're drinking Psychedelic
Cat Grass makes you woozy yet your dream
is real   the nether self the apple that
you pluck your passion dance   your bangles dangle
shrunken heads yes moons as well as suns

candle

the avant artist in my earbuds bleats
i love her love her love her love her skirls
of skronky feedback urban hunter drums
a cagefree angel slinging every third
verse to infinitude // not theft but re
appropriation of the blues cold beer
goes well with it & my own wordswordswords
their only referent my selves // you find me
in the dimness of this office loft
& lose me in the black pool of my mind
like Hamlet's solipsistic twin i talk
too much should listen more to women in
my life i've filled up thirteen junk drawers in
this house you say one candle's all i need

chamber tragicomedy

it's Wagner's *Tristan* streaming from the kitchen
speaker   potent ale in front of me
i think about the tragic arc the way
it mimics amplifies the life of those
who strive & die   a cis male fantasy
perhaps   //   i've striven most of my adult
life to avoid an easy self-importance
yet insisted on my mantra *all things*
end in sadness for so goddamn long
that you exhaustedly agree   //   night's fallen
blackened branches foreground blacker sky
i hear dark laughter thundering between
the stars then echoing within my heart
or is it just the dishwasher's dull slosh

chrome attic

the color's in your head of course with dust
& bats last generation's mattresses
// in one old house you lived in college days
unfinished attic with a mattress sex
there several times oh hot as hell no not
the sex // you have a good friend who wears only
black but you're more into color nuance
ain't your jam oh smelling purple hearing
orange tasting blue there's synesthesia
of the psyche too // in Poe the house
is metaphor for head the corpse below
the floorboards won't stay dead // chrome attic so
unnatural it shines too easy mirror
stained by things that needn't even touch it

close to home

cold beer in front of me & black dog at
my feet // my wife's on Zoom pro football's on
the muted mega screen tv // routine
has morphed me to a chimpanzee who irons
his own shirts // the music in my earbuds
good but too damn smooth Rachmaninov
// behooves me to beware delusion not sure
where these words came from can't weaponize
them yet // the poet that i'm reading says
she cannot write the lovely kinds of poems
her schooling trained her in // ah well the darkest
path is close to home // the what & how
& when & god yes why mean next to nothing
who am i & where do i belong

cruel month

a Hamlet sky this morning undecided
rain at noon fruit trees in bloom the sex
of pollen in my eyes   i love this time
of year the beauty & the terror   //   use
or lose day off i kill time listening
to bootlegged Dylan albums lambs' blood in
his voice   //   the spruces sway like mastodons
time's wheel's turned prehistoric could be any
era   human suffering's the same
// oh Tom relax my darker angel says
you know the up-close view is tragic   praise
the Fates that you're not weepy   wimpy maybe
ask your mom oh snap she's dead   you look
like her at least you haven't grown a beard

the deal

this evening's dogwalk   springlike light & pubic
grass   i moped all day in brain fog now
i feel my rebel hormones   wounded band
of siblings   coming to   //   this May i'm turning
sixtyfour   an earworm Beatles tune's
tamped down by gauzy rags of dream   six fingered
hands that cut a Tarot deck i love
the pictures never get the meaning   //   that's
the deal my darker angel tells me   sorrow
loss regret departure   friendship drunken
dancing rowing on the moonlit river
all mixed willynilly   //   backyard spruces
sway in soft breeze   three times taller than
they were twelve years ago   they too will die

decluttering

we've moved old furniture downstairs faux leather
chairs brocade upholstered bench stacked dishware
we can give away the handmade artfair
masks & ornaments we've tired of
// decluttering my wife's obsession yes
i get it we are made more beautiful
by loss i'm not sure that's her thought i stole
it from a poet // dinner with some friends
at six i've found a decent claret in
the pantry to regift // i'd love to write
a poem today these darkened jottings psychic
data points can i relate them to
a larger world // clouds gathering i hope
it rains still love the clutter it creates

the demon dynamo

my parents built a teenage bedroom for me
in the basement of the house i slept
& lifted weights played hard & punk rock music
loud // the roof of Hell my parents walked
& bore of course dark shadows of their own
but i believe i was the über shadow
of the house the demon dynamo
// my homie angel tells me that's poetic
puffery & has me sipping tea
instead of swilling beer a Zim who's into
Zen // but i cling hard to western shit
i so revere the sixties baseball cards
the eighties zines with poems of mine no one
should read these burn like kindling in my mind

ether

tonight i feel ethereal my mind
pours ether on a cloth to press against
my thoughts // dog sleeping at my feet he's such
a baby like my only living son
the fire glows warm against my face & hands
the lacing in my beer glass Great Lakes foam
in goldbrown light // as if the chronicles
of sadness have been captured on a final
scroll that we're committing to the fire
we burn the past imagining a finite
puff of sparkling smoke we know we know
it's only smoke // a string quartet is streaming
now the bows bright blades that scrape the ice
of heaven wet snow dying in the flames

étude

the dog & you are lying in the living
room   a golden evening sun outside
no need to light the fireplace   //   it's Glass's
Études for Piano in your headphones
makes you pensive   maybe it's the beer
or pressure of mortality   you dream
you're with the compost at the curb you try
to settle down & track the actual
then find the crack in it that lets the real
& healing light seep in   //   last midnight while
you kissed your lover's thighs you thought of what
a poet said   to write a poem dip
a bucket in the hidden river of
the psyche see what nourishment comes up

fever

the pasta water rocks the pot you smell
hot wood   a string quartet is sawing pine
boards from your speakers for your coffin nighttime
presses like a succubus its thighs
& breasts befog then frost the plate glass door
//   your dog lies snoring black as Cerberus
& all the walls glow pomegranate   pale
you hunker well below the roof of Hell
& ride a bucking fever that you dearly
love those ember eyes in snowy dark
//   you want to wrestle Satan or whichever
demon you've been overfeeding but
your thoughts are cracking fast as April ice
your soul is swinging like a pendulum

the fire within

the windswept night yawns wide so much like me
the cosmos weary of existence all
it seems gets broken on the wheel the tree
that binds this world the blinding suns that fall
then rise then fall // the coasts recede the seas
devour as they swell unconsciousness
ascendant human frailty on its knees
but worshiping a misplaced power // bless
the fire within the evermounting flame
the third eye open wide the living flesh
we press in joy in need // the world we frame
revolves & is resolved forever fresh
in us so gaze at the horizon find
the faintest star all fits inside the mind

flat rusty blood

so what's inside the psyche's bucket   rust
distortions & contortions portions of
a self   no   selves   an angel that my old
friend William calls the anima   //   the abstract
painting in the dining room it's dated 63
Dave's brother Fred did it at Yale   untitled
i call it *flat rusty blood* just love
its menstrual swirls   //   those folk punk rockers post
punk gothers on the stereo i think
of scars that hold back blood & lips that hold
back words   no   worlds   the fires in the sky
three trillion miles away give little warmth
but tantalizing light   my angel bites
my lip with every kiss i lick the scab

for a while

it's Mozart in the car Bob Dylan at
the gym   strong coffee in the morning bitter
beer at night   my meds i like to say
but i am just a dilettante of grief
//   white sunshine through the blinds a black dog at
my feet & you here with me reading this
the whole thing's comic we're just passing through
it all comes down to attitude or stance
//   i pet the dog his silken head   he shakes
his floppy ears & hops up on all fours
i take a bite of cheeseburger give him
a piece   you say that i'm his dad   //   i feel
a smile that stretches past my manufactured
angst   i think i'll stay here for a while

grace space

oh let me live it first & not just in
my head but with my body breathing corpse
that dances for the gods though i don't see it
only scribbles highlife hieroglyphs
& once true runes // a phone call from my angel
changes everything of course i'm too
much boy to check for orphic voicemail that
could save me // lifetimes working like a devil
for a taste of heaven dreams to age
with grace create a clean lit place a vigil
for my individuality
// flames flicker sanguinary amber lemon
then reverse i beg my better self
for clemency cry treat me as a ~~fiend~~ friend

husband's hash

today the pale gold sunlight in the greening
trees your too warm fleece   you kissed your wife
before you left for work while she was trimming
woody shrubs that blocked the dog's path to
the porch steps   ambiguity is what
you read behind her glasses   eyes within
a petri dish examined from the bottom
data points a scatterplot your life
//   & during fleeting happiness those flecks
of colored light   each face you see a petal
beautiful and mortal   daughter &
her mother   dip your bucket down the river
is the same   & ever-changing   bring
the trembling ladle to your mouth & taste

the inks

remember when i worked toward good those days
a river deeds like salmon leaping boulders
levees many bitter beers ago
// a jet roars overhead can i come back
of course you can my angel sings *but just*
not all the way // i carry water in
the desert more than metaphor the poet
that i'm reading says a pulley lifts
us up to heaven i still think about
deep wells beneath // you tell me that the things
we do mean everything & nothing both
are true the tattooed moon we're drinking booze
the bloodlet dawn the coffee's on fuck death
indelible the inks that staining us sustain

listen to me

the coins worn well beyond denomination
still hold value borrowed stolen begged for
melted down for slag   //   just think abstract
yes honor hatred love complacency
what Ezra called obscenities   but concrete
detail earns their use   say jack pines blackened
in the shadows   fingers warmed by pen
farfalle bubbling hard in Thumper   Dad's
old pasta pot   //   can i say something hopeful
for a poem that i'm fretting over   art's
a force yes even when we force it   //   *ford*
the stream that eats the dead men's faces   dip
your bucket in & spill it   sings the muse
i love you when you listen to me Zim

minor key

wet walk in dripping woods this morning brown
leaves slippery underfoot   two cups of coffee
coursing through my body's sullen channels
Trey hunched snuffling Ann controlled the leash
& i took poop patrol   our allegory
//   now it's Mozart on the stereo
i've finished a Bukowski book i wasn't
wild about & Ashbery is next
dissimilar familiars haunting nonetheless
//   the backyard spruces darken with the weather
like my psyche loving minor scales
my keyboard's dusty with disuse how can
that be   the skylight's beaded all the world's
on fire with rain i'm drowning in its flames

nocturne (vii)

your father's dead but haunts like Hamlet's dad
while indecision slips its noose around
your neck   *to kill to die to live*   forgive
the banshees incubi & succubi
that gallop through your sleep // the morning's sticky
sigil on your bedsheet   prepubescent
prayer nothing ever came of it
career of evil thwarted too   your fear
of punishment & plain old death // & now
your smile is cracked the meds you hoard all week
don't dull your pain night's pentimento bleeds
through every daybreak darkening your father's
barnyard   starlit knives & pitchfork coal-black
billygoat that whispers   lambs that cry

old daze

venetian blinds moonlit your belly sliced
like bread // before though kisses traded rassling
in the weedy lot behind the Beef Days
Ferris wheel // we bummed a ride back home
Cheap Trick Bob Seger playing loud inside
the F-10 cab yes we were stacked in back
with tarps scrap metal sparking when we tossed it
on the highway singing "I Fought the Law"
// then homeward you & i my arm slung cross
your shoulders drunken broken orphic such
was my delusion // notebook out i scribbled lines
a sonnet "College Daze" you poured the drinks
bikini line the border guarded no
i met you at the great divide alive

poor pilgrim

eyes ears nose mouth these body parts i squeak
so clean // the windows to the world of things
& no ideas but there one poet says
another writes that there's an ear within
the genitals a one eyed bear between
the legs // allusions dog my brainspace windows
floor to ceiling where i sit // eyes are
the windows to the soul i heard that from
my mother first & thinking of her smooths
my thought i think // were she alive i'd write
her this *in sun in snow in ebb & flow*
the passions in & out the window go
time's thievery a beggar man's belief
poor pilgrim isn't love worth all the grief

pressure cooker

so nothing much external needs to happen
since the braincase is a pressure cooker
with a lid that loosely fits // & me
i'm channeling Great Uncle Walt just simmering
simmering simmering oh so close
to boiling // thank my reading & my weird
friends look even doggo's panting at
my feet dishwasher churning like
a biplane spiraling on fire // psyche's
chasm charm a Mariana Trench
a million buckets to dip in spill out
// oh see & smell nay feel the fragrant steam
that's nimbusing my muse stoked lobster red
claws tap tap tapping hissing into song

retro listening

i listen retro regularly   Joy
Division Gang of Four i find the essence
rare   we share this world with younger punks
sad vampires biting hunks   a windmill's slicing
wrists & necks   no   that's the dishwasher
its second cycle third who knows   like crazy
Yeats & all his gyres twerking art
& history a looped infinity
//   the dog is panting could be me a hazy
sky without rain's satisfaction   dusk
just dropped its purple drawers i haven't even
cracked a beer & through the kitchen window
i see mastodons   no   shaggy spruces
record spinning backwards black as day

scatterplot

i thumb my notebook finger dusty keys
i dived a dolphin dreaming // now awake
// my energy & outlook brighten with
the sunlit day // i seek core samples from
my psyche // images are memories
the meter is my breathing & my pulse
// the window that i face a canvas stretched
the screen a tablet to be etched // these lines
thin tributaries branching from my dark
& hidden river // dip the bucket in
again my muse cajoles // each finished poem
a data point a dot to place upon
my scatterplot the everchanging ghostly
shape of what i make with this brief life

science fiction

i watch a remixed sci fi classic on
tv while munching chips & letting a
new poem marinate // oh subterfuge
& centrifuge unconscious slow deluge
i'm thinking of the mushy middle of
the book i'm editing & Dad also
a sci fi fan dead all these years how booze
& age had softened him // the ale i'm drinking
hits me hard the movie picks up steam
with maker myths the villain's existential
angst more interesting than our hero's
struggle with his work & distant lover
// don't need Daedalus to be reminded
even great men father foolish sons

space to cross

so many years ago a drinking buddy
told me of a night when he lay staring
at the stars just crying at their beauty
sensitivity that shamed me i
who never has to cry do you // he brewed
his own beer in the basement of his house
a trap door in the kitchen floor he had
a crazy spouse like me i never lose
my brainy cool do you // these secret vital
darknesses the breaking through the crossing
over messages like falcon shadows
on the thunderheads oh friend if you
can't find the space you must create it &
if you can find the threshold you must cross it

string theory

pro football on tv so Ann on Zoom
& Trey a nightblack Cerberus at my feet
a bath today so he's half traumatized
// the string quartet that's playing saws my heart's
taut strings string theory of the cosmos silken
ties of love that bind // this atmosphere
within my mind perceived reality
faint data points recorded by the senses
analyzed so blindly here // imagine
artists sitting circled round a flame
suspended moonlit mist surrounds it could
be snow it could be ashes of a god
on fire // the art of others startles tears
from us emotions new unnameable

tender green

not money though you love it dearly not
as much as grass & trees & sunlit seas
asparagus like neon hair of earth
// oh leaves & dollars bitcoins spores all wealth
ephemerality // our words just crude
translations of our things our poems crude
translations of our lives // you feel the rivers
streaming underneath your skin you think
of old Thoreau comparing his hand to
a fallen leaf or Frost with nothing gold
that stays or Ginsberg's sensitive bullshit
// oh only beauty makes you cry but booze
& age have softened you to tenderness
beyond what your imagined culture bears

to a poet i know

this data from the senses scratchy throat
snow drifting down like ashes angel feathers
sticking in the spruces whine of tires
on the interstate // an Amazon
delivery the squealing brakes & on
the radio a pop song you don't know
// emotion that's the sixth sense it's a theory
anyway how do you feel the world
just doesn't care so you should do your work
// your memories the reconstruction of
the past your mother's it'll happen if
it's meant to be your father's whodathunkit
// time plus these your found materials
oh what you do with it is up to you

II.
Range

ash

increasingly
i think
i understand

the motivation
of those artists
great & small

whose work's designedly
impermanent

reminds me
of what Leonard Cohen said

that if your life is burning
well
the poetry is just
the ash

being made

your favorite rock 'n' roll band's gotten old
yes older than the dead & distant stars

whose light you see tonight   a hundred years
to get here   like the other dead you see

in dreams or under whiskey's smoky spell
//   you say your better self is lying on

the foldout sofa bed   your wife's upstairs
your needy dog will find you yet   there on

the ottoman the books you've stolen from
//   great leaders   sausages   you love them both

but couldn't bear to see them being made
each maker rides a horse that nags them to

infinity   your shadow & your breathing
corpse   Venn diagram in flux   dependent

on a streetlight   moon   or sun   your forebears
doppelgängers   ghostly pentimento

bony shoulders

a setting sun with broken clouds
three sisters grim & spinning with you
as you write another entry in your cursed record
how much wasted life

your self help angel (former flagellant) advises
talk to your own wicked self
as if it were your fiend
your friend i mean

too cozy to embrace
you roll your die of life six faces
Love Art Sex
Death Death & Death

you don't trust happiness
balloon snagged in a thorn tree
money only pads life's corners
daggers everywhere

an old friend's sick
so smart & sensitive
but fending off sure death
the die keeps rolling on its bony shoulders

Dada moves (ii)

dewed sagas

nun poop deified
rotator madam solos
civic stats redder

*

jung wife

stories half i
there's a don't somewhere

*

kook level pep reviver

boob dewed solos toot
repaper sagas redder
dad poop deified

*

of course

quivering with revelation,
shouts, "Millard Fillmore!"

*

oh too

am i who
happens so weird

*

rivière bleue

singing under the skin of her thigh

*

sinatra mantra

lost vegas vast logos

*

stash variations

Dali dolly dally
lady laid laddy daily
dada la di da

the door

oh angel we

our fraught adjoining selves

were separated
by a door

that fate
or someone you or i
had locked

*

so like that cage
i welded stoutly
in another life

i bloodied nails
on that damned door
between us

i who thought myself
a conduit a harbinger
an acolyte
of life

& you whom i believed
to be its corresponding
equal opposite
yes death

oh this was my belief

*

you took a chainsaw
to that door

you're practical & like
things clean & tidy

nearly cutting through

*

i broke
the rest down with my hands
the jamb & hinges too

we pieced the door together
use it as our dinner table now

& i'm no longer sure
what i believe

enlightenment

red kitchen lights above
Atlantic blue dusk creeping down outside

a bitter ale in front of you
your wife scrolls through her phone

dog stares you down
he wants a snack

desires & needs
these mammal drives

you scratch behind your ear
& sniff what's ready for the compost
orange peels curled on the counter
coffee grounds with soggy filter
wilted butter lettuce from last week
& someday
you

& now that thud you sometimes hear
you're sure a songbird
flying free
has hit the window glass
oh will it live

tonight
enlightenment is just like this

equinox

a rainy dogwalk after two dry weeks so coats & pants all wet
laid out like corpses in the entryway

keep thinking of our ornamental maple dead i killed it with a
pruning too enthusiastic this past spring you don't agree

but now it's football season stretched out on the sofa book of
poems   Gary Snyder love his work   laid open on my chest i
watch the Lions then the Saints the tv muted other music in my
head

my midday coffee midlife crisis not sure who i am or how i feel i
worry that this doesn't worry me

in silent drizzle little yellow leaves are falling like confetti

from a nightmare notebook (ii)

autumn revenant

no matter how i carve
the jack o lantern
cracks your smile

*

goth wedding

hazy blood moon
your opioid
dissolving in dark rum

the heady chalice cracks
you are hers
mere thing hereafter

*

legendary

drunken poet drowns
embracing harvest moon
reflected in the river

haiku for my muse

murmurs in the fog
bedsheets swirling on the line
searching for your ghost

the hidden springs

dead half the year   those smoke-gray days i think
i'm broken on the wheel of fate   a fool
in borrowed robes   but not today   blue sky
bright sun   dew sparkling underfoot   i drink
the light   to nourish my own darkness   pool
the hidden springs that murmur *this is i*

ice cream headache

we talked about the concrete & abstract the way you earn the abstract by portraying the concrete   it demonstrates your care/ desire to find a common ground it says you pay attention   //   i prefer to talk instead of listen i am notably unwise my fellow poet KD agrees with one or both of these   post post ironic this   //   it takes me back to Mom & Dad ironic family dinners all that i can do is laugh into my water glass absurdity of it all   the things Mom puts in pasta sauce like pork chops drumsticks bones & all & at the Dairy Queen we're sitting in the car Dad puts his bare feet on the dashboard wiggles his long toes starts singing rooty toot toot   i eat too fast bad ice cream headache see so clearly now that life will last too long

ice water gurgles
into drowned bard's cowl of froth
head severed   singing

matters gray & dark

the dog & i have just come back from our
slow trot through dappled sun & shade   much like
my better self & i slipstreaming through

this life   lightheaded & beguiled   in someone
else's mind   //   now fed & petted he's
Anubis   jackal god canopic jar lid

comatose in minutes flat   & i
will burn this Sunday   mummified like Ramses
on the leather sofa   dozing through

a horror film   then evening meds   two black
& bitter beers   //   oh so much more there is
to this dark world   to matters gray & dark

the poet that I'm reading wants to kiss
his great grandmother's pubic bone   the dead
crowd all around us   telling me they're me

1977

experimental cornfield
—yes that is a thing—
breathes right across
the street

new high school over
rolling hills
a little farther south

your teenage basement bedroom
posters 8 tracks albums
Pink Floyd Kiss Led Zeppelin

gigantic German radio
like something from the war

suntanned summer girlfriend
condoms in
your dad's sock drawer

Oktoberfest

you're on your second six
the dog's blurred third head snores

dishwasher's sea of darkness
roars of shorter days
& weaker sun

yet still the fiery wheel
you're broken on

regrets you've savored
for their piquancy
now stretch as bland as sands
of Ozymandias

oh cursed be you
to try to find lost time

you're lying mummified
in middle age
with laundry tub
recycling bin
canopic jars

the backyard evergreens
bend under dusk's
gray ash

as gray as
every morning's shaved off beard
gone swirling swiftly
down the drain
with all the wisdom
it supposedly confers

Sage

a cloudy warm & muggy car commute
you're singing with the CD playing *oh*
my sweet Lafayette Lucinda Williams
sparks your memory job interview
that Cajun drummer had the hots for you
// & now out back bra off & beer in hand
you see that iris swaying like a spider
in the purple dusk // so many dusks
in front of you you grab another beer
write *Mom kept Dad's leash awfully tight two beers*
a night your penmanship has gone to crap
oh what the hell a sexist lexicon
// you worry that the intern you misgendered
by mistake today will tell HR
a long career of kindness balances
accounts in heaven surely here // you check
the bowtie pasta it's al dente toss
in herbs & wilted greens show them who's boss

a slice of the sublime

it's Bruckner in my headphones
beer beside me
doggo too
my wife on Zoom

& after daylong clouds
the sun i swear
it speaks to me

oh angel
i will never tire of this

how could i ever
stop believing
that this world is mine

tall corn

we're at the drive-in movie
'65 Impala
Mom & Dad
Jean Chris & i
three horror films

it's Corman
Hammer
Night of the Living Dead

tall cornfields breathing all
around us
in the dark

Mom's cigarette tinged laughter
smells of death

Dad
bare feet on the dashboard
wiggling his toes

apparently alive

these words obscene

you love your excess
bourbon scotch
the thought of sex

they make you loco though
so you're King Lear again
yes running naked in the woods
your bat & balls flop-flopping freely

it's too early for the stars
that rivet night's black armor
for the comet that will strike
the pale blue marble

madness has a mortgage on your body
bloody lien upon your soul

so find the art in your distemper
your oppression
your old howling blue eyed blues

go search the world for mercy
beauty justice truth
these words obscene
in poetry & maybe even life
unless you use them right

i never could

the tower

within the tower
of the heart a
hunchback pulls
the bell rope   some
impossible beloved's
near but distanced
by brute fact
imagination's lack
//   the square below
a chessboard's
chiaroscuro prison
bishop knight &
rook   weak king
fresh captured queen
string up the poet
kook who'll die for
beauty   //   unmoved
gods laugh darkly
at the quarking chaos
in the cosmos   death
beats art for now
a ragged cloud
obscures the
waxing moon

why hold onto ashes

a line of storms
rolled through this afternoon
those hoofbeats

thump my inner ear tonight
blood music that
the damned can dance to

yes i've cracked a beer
& like a chuck roast
i am stewing in my juices

bubbles steam
& troubled dreams
we're all so lightly here

this triple chin is just
the slippage of my masks
a ruse that rubs off youth

& doggo my old fanged familiar
black as Acheron
he stares me down

i wipe the fogged up window
see a doppelgänger looking back at me
& then another shroud of steam

& there's a wife
that fits in here somewhere
i swear

i burn i burn with life
these words spooked crows
a fluttering residue

increasingly i understand
those artists making works
designedly impermanent

why hold onto ashes
from creation's fire
live love transform move on

III.
Angels

ambrosias

oh Bernstein's Mahler 4 sounds great
& Thumper
Dad's old pasta pot
is straining
toward its name

tonight i'm way too weird
for a dinner date with friends
my wife she feels it
takes one for the team

there's football on tv
dishwasher churns
the dog & i don't mind

the daylong wind's died down

this bitter beer
my kitchen Buddha
squats and sweats

this fleeting Now
the best i've felt all day

i've found a new place to dwell

these memories of Dad & Mom
heirloom tomatoes that i slice
it's not Dad's knife

& Mahler on the playlist
all this beauty overripe

*

so Mom
loved blue
her mother cooked for parish priests
two brothers boxing champs
somewhere in there
a kernel
me

good dancer
Elvis fan
her smoker's kisses
tasted just the way
that i've imagined death

when you feel you need to

it's Klemperer's Beethoven 5
this catnap afternoon

the roof guys come & gone
such thunder

now i pray
no wait
for rain

i've got three pens lined up
the blue ones for my words
the red one for my mind

the lamp bulb is a dying sun
the power cord's umbilical's lukewarm

the poet that I'm reading says
the sky can't get up
off the ground

sometimes it's best
to just lie down

questions from the sofa bed

my cell phone off
the tv muted
open book of verse facedown
not saying whose

my better self is lying
quietly
& neither dog nor sleep
has found me yet

who is that movie star
Mom loved her so

and what's that neighbor's
big dog's name
my wife she knows

how old's Mick Jagger
i've begun to see my dad in me

who said that leaders are like sausages
we don't like seeing either made

skull session

i meant to write a poem today
but too hungover

it's ok

these scattered storms
this abstract music in my head

a crazy quilt's
on top of me
my wife's mom made it

memories & propositions
glaze & crackle
in the kiln's white heat

the years spent trying ways
to straighten things

oh what does Hamlet say
let be

finders keepers triptych

1

the swirling mist
the twisted bedsheets on the line
still searching for you
angel   ghost

2

pale raven
linger
blueeyed soul torchsinger

oh i write this in the middle
of the piddling night
the ac keeps my thin skin cool
it has a valve for grief
but i'm on fire fire fire

3

your body is
an ocean
i
am chained to
its night tides

rocksteady

half comatose below the ceiling fan
i smell the neighbors' lilacs
blossoms popping on the fruit trees
also barbecue
almost kickstarts my flagging heart

so tell me moodster
what's your mode
oh baby baby
poor poor me

yes it's my coin toss angel
kisskissquizzing me
oh how i've missedmissedmissed it

Zeppelin wailing on your work commute
& Pink Floyd for your doppelbock
mocktragic nights

rocksteady loser
oh I burn
with love for you
afraid that you might win

after a wet walk in dripping woods

oh the psyche's sullen channels
we remember feelings
but forget
the concrete details
that they're set within

a thumbed Bukowski
stuffed back on the shelf
last night's pulled pork
tubbed chilling in the fridge

i can't imagine
Mozart's keyboard
ever being dusty

thus this journal
my paroxysms
start off cool blue
but get their color back
within
the pale vagina
of it

with barrel aged ale

it's Mahler's 2nd in my headphones
wife on Zoom with friends
the tortellini cooked
the postgame muted on tv
checkcheck   checkcheck

& i am reading
Ashbery's unfinished
poems

gives the reader
lots of space

i sack
my word hoard
my whored words

is anything i've ever written any good

relax
don't push
my burnt end angel sings

diminishing returns

day misty   gray   so much like me

Beethoven's 4th
a bashful sister
streaming through the kitchen

bedsheets in the washer
dog is zonked
the coffee's gone

read on I dare you
last night's journal rant
page 7 three beers in

i've burned through many lives
to earn my ironies
the words just ash

& here's my wine stained angel
with a proto ancient prompt

come on Prometheus
the mud is drying

yet another life

Sisyphean

four cups of coffee
Haydn in my headphones

slept in late
been reading poetry
then watching football
reading poetry
my playlist on repeat

all from the situation room
my mancave couch

& though they darken
lighten
darken
backyard spruces
keep their green all year

i think about Camus
& repetition's beautiful
with symmetry
its variations meaningful
homemade
a dash of dissonance
thrown in

familiars

dark river deep within me
big black bag i drag around
sweet ache of sentience

the metaphors familiar
& now for the quotidian

i'm in the moonless woods with doggo
headlamp catches
or creates
a pair of eerie neon green coyote
fox or deer or
something
eyes

oh beauty
& its mother
Death

i see my breath
i'm giving birth
to ghosts   to angels   i—

mountain mover

a mountain mover
drunk & listening to delta music
so i style myself

appalled by age's ravages
but slogging on
with death & debt
our kissing inbred cousins
vying for my brainspace

rambling's on my mind
but stones are in my passway
blues truth twanging in my ears

*

misterioso memories of wilderness

black howling wolves
in predawn Tetons woods

Montana mountain goats
ablur on crags like ghostly snow

pent phosphorescent sulfur springs
bub bubbling hot at Yellowstone

my wife sticks with me
better worse sickness health it's hard to tell

the devil lurking somewhere too

but that's God's watch
not yours
my Roundhead angel purrs
a Puritan
in secret wants to wear
my soft red pants

*

bad altar boy i was
a back pew sniggerer
who worked the weekday masses only
rode the pine on Sundays

i remember Father Deere
guy's name i swear it
telling us
the odds are better with belief
no God & you lose nothing
when you die
if he exists though
jackpot
in the afterlife

hurt heroes striving broken on the wheel of fate
oh tragedy's a cis male fantasy

the poet that i'm reading wants to die
at least the people in her poems do
they themselves are Hell
& she herself is dead

the work however
screams
i am alive i am alive

pale riders

my little sister's just turned sixty one
insurance claim adjuster long retired
yikes
like yesterday it seems
McCombs Park merry go round
timefrozen redbrick jr high
with Inky the crow
the truant smokers' chosen mascot

let be be finale of seem
oh bless you
necessary
anal retentive
angel

all of this is true
it's just not factual

*

the symphony i listen to
Weinberg
a rediscovery
draws blood
with brass & drums
pale riders in the mud

i'm thinking of the many muggy hikes
much like today's

my shadow Trey & i
three stooges in the dappled woods
where i discovered nothing much
the smell of rain
detention pond white heron
shoes dew soaked a fifth straight day

my glasses sliding down my nose i push them up
& down they go i push them up
old Sisyphean hope in private Hades

*

cloudy sky thick mist right now
the music darkens too
violas cellos basses moaning
it's an elegy
alive with blessings fits of anguish
these the world knows well
we enter crying what should we expect

a fly is buzzing at the pane
blue uncertain stumbling
roaring high a 737
giant silver crucifix

oh Emily oh Tomas
dear dead poets
helping haunting
yes i owe you big time
think of all the books i'll sell

two bluesmen

two bluesmen on the stereo
yes one repeats the other's verses

could be repetitious perfectly unbearable
but variations
in the sound & rhythm of the voices
make it beautiful   to me at least

& Thumper   Dad's old pasta pot
is rattling
burner up on high   like Lucifer

& now my darker maybe brighter angel
sometimes i can't tell lovelove them both
pipes in
remember what your dying father said
i should have spent two dollars
yes for every one i saved
i did the opposite i got it wrong

oh Dad i'm here
have not directly tried to kill myself
or any other

one thing right
one thing   write

dancing madly backwards

i'm posing in the mirror
idiot hero of my household
bare forked animal ahowling   better so
euphoria a drying brushstroke
on the fresco of my psyche

man boobs
clucks my angel with the tummy tuck
yes wearing something tight again
just what i like
you're no Mick Jagger
more like Mr Jiggles

yes the price of not yet having died

time wrinkles back to high school best friend Brett
too cool for me & into weird shit loved ELP & Tull
on Beaker Street a band called Captain Beyond

too much upper body move your feet
instructs my mother 1975
her menthol cig on fire
Elvis fan good dancer
helps me get my groove on

all my life been moving fast
so no one else can find the places where i rest

the desperate quotidian

mid ’60s Coltrane on the stereo
the gyro meat well cooked
my second book no sales on Amazon
lies facedown on a tv tray

the house remodel blues
my wife unboxes & inspects
a tall new toilet
barstools on backorder

haven’t even cracked a beer
oh soon my love

*

another night
one part sublime
the rest the desperate quotidian

left knee still killing me
right shoulder crackling like puffed rice
& later when we’re naked
doggo eyes us with disdain

this getting old
there’s not much good about it

wisdom
ha

*

oh leave a record Zimmy
prove you've been alive
although it's for the reader to decide

yes that's my comp lit angel
into Derrida
so doesn't trust the author

fine
but just who reads this shit
professor shaman charlatan el stinko poet
penitent who gibbers to a god
that isn't there

sometimes i wish my poems would just click shut

i guess i should feel free
take flight ignite or dive
hell burrow underground
for thirteen years
emerge red eyed

it's more than metaphor
attempted self
transcendence

i—i—

angel dear
did you just fart

the cycles

the ducks & geese
the coming north the going south
teenager crying in the bathroom
menstrual cramps

my wife reminds me men have cycles too
i'm so erratic i'm not sure
the drugs & muses help of course

the visible horizon
right now windblown trees blue sky
fits comfortably inside my mind
but it's my lifetime's arc
because i'm in its midst
that i can't see

oh man that's half baked acid Zen
yes that's my roach clip angel
dreamy kisser
likes badmouthing me

our happiness will come & go
balloon snagged in the mind's own razor wire

but the stone
the restless waters swirl around
is
(mouth it angel)
(i can't get no) satisfaction

my brighter maybe darker angel sings

so you hear sawing humming
smell fresh pine boards for a coffin

oh relax it's just a string quartet the end of time
that's streaming through your headphones

how you love the mind to leap
ascend to yonder blue
or dive into the darkest pool
above below inside beyond
the soul's extremes are what you seek

don't pause hit play
such themes & variations
aural memes for meaningful creation

later when the tracks play through
just breathe look back at your small tracks
the human trace
that tells your fellow wanderers
that you were here

& look
your sometime lover leather sofa homemade quilt

you've found yourself
not quite alone

Mr Cinnamon

road burning with wrong turns
wrong ways dead ends & do not enters
rain's far off but coming

home my wife & i
out hoeing weeds and spreading mulch
it's tiring mildly pleasant
like my manchild life

my true groove yes   or is it rut
is working out
how my quotidian can swallow
nausea & ennui

oh i'm still learning
don't complain
be grateful
act
move on
a mantra list
i've stolen from a poet
that i haven't read in years

*

this evening finally
we're drinking beer out on the deck

my image in the backdoor glass
i suck my gut in puff my chest

& doggo curled up like an Alien beside us
burgers sizzling on the grill

squirrel chitters in the spruces
blue smoke hanging there so ghostly

citronella mortadella Louis vamping Ella
hell let's let the damned mosquitoes feed

you're sensitive as a side of beef
yes that's my free range angel
tongue burnt sucking icicles in Hell
so can't pronounce my name
& calls me Mr Cinnamon
that's Cin for short

*

i shake my gory locks
my psyche's no black box

i hear my wife my angel that old cornball Satan
plead
Cin dip a bucket in your darkest river
spill it out
on me at least

the poet that i'm reading says
that genius lives in troubled minds

& mine
has rediscovered
i'm in love

Appendix

advice about advice

the poet that i'm reading offers this advice
one   don't complain
two   count your blessings
three   do what you can   take action
four move on   the mind's ongoing

this sounds good to me

the poem's entitled *Garbage*[1] though
perhaps i'm missing some key irony

this poem that i'm reading you right now
"advice about advice"
is surely missing something key as well

*

ChatGPT?!

it's advice about advice
is seven smoothshod homilies
for one   just who's the person giving you advice
two's   context matters
three's   beware of certainty
four says   advice is no command
just use it or discard it
as you would a tool

dear Tom i think i'm gonna barf
don't let a bot replace your thought

that's my critical thinking angel   fidgets in my head
i'm guessing you all have one too
it's sorta like a conscience
with a sense of humor

bless you angel
i will mend my ways

*

Psychology Today[3] has offered up 3 Rs
no not the ones that school's imprinted on our brains
these instead are tips for acting on advice
review   make sure you understand the context
reframe   make sure it fits your needs
respond   take action

Harvard Business[4] says
advice is hard on both the giver & receiver
flawed logic & a scarcity of information
trip us up

*

oh where to go

i asked my wife Ann
for advice about advice

smooth move dear Tom
you really think you have a shot
at husband of the year

sassy very sassy
love you angel dear

Ann mentioned Tara Mohr[5]
who offers these 3 Rs
(have all of us been traumatized by school?!)
to help evaluate advice
reframing
relevance
revising
bottom line   advice is more about the person giving it

also Daniel Pink[6]
whose view is rosier

i hear my angel groaning

Pink says "asking for advice creates a partner"

*

writers are my *psychic* partners

here is Cicero[7]
no one can give you better advice than yourself

Ben Franklin[8] says
wise men don't need advice
& fools won't take it

Edna St. Vincent Millay[9]
please give me some good advice
i promise not to take it

Tom they're getting sleepy very very sleepy
let the other crackpots
have a chance to talk

the journey
like this poem
is unfinishable

we take the journey
till the journey takes us

ah bless you angel
sweet remembrancer

beloved fellow travelers
awake!

Faculty Address
Washtenaw Community College Commencement Ceremony
Eastern Michigan University
17 May 2025

***

Sources

1. A.R. Ammons, *Garbage*, W.W. Norton & Company, 1994, p. 55.
2. https://chatgpt.com/c/6822701e-52ac-8007-ad9c-eea08b71f0d6, 12 May 2024.
3. https://www.psychologytoday.com/us/blog/connected-leadership/202301/how-to-listen-to-advice-and-act-accordingly#:~:text=It's%20important%20to%20be%20objective,well%20as%20to%20other%20people.
4. https://hbr.org/2015/01/the-art-of-giving-and-receiving-advice
5. Notes from Tara Mohr's "Unhooking from Praise and Criticism," Playing Big Facilitator Training, 28 Mar. 2023.
6. Daniel Pink, https://www.linkedin.com/feed/update/urn:li:activity:7324796674336350208/?updateEntityUrn=urn%3Ali%3Afs_updateV2%3A%28urn%3Ali%3Aactivity%3A7324796674336350208%2CFEED_DETAIL%2CEMPTY%2CDEFAULT%2Cfalse%29
7. Cicero https://www.brainyquote.com/topics/advice-quotes
8. Ben Franklin https://www.brainyquote.com/topics/advice-quotes
9. Edna St. Vincent Millay https://www.brainyquote.com/topics/advice-quotes

Creative Extremists

"The nation and the world are in dire need
of creative extremists."
These words are from Martin Luther King Jr's
"Letter from Birmingham Jail."

Let's fast-forward to 1976,
thirteen years after King wrote his great Letter
and only eight years after his death.

1976 was not only the year of our nation's bicentennial
I remember my dad grew a beard to celebrate it;
he looked like Abraham Lincoln.

But 1976 was also the year,
legend has it,
that a handful of WCC English instructors
knocked down a wall
—talk about breaking barriers!—
on the third floor of this very building
to create WCC's first Writing Center,
something they knew the College and its students needed.

What were these feisty latter-day-hippie instructors
if not creative extremists?

In his Letter, King names
some of history's notable creative extremists,
writing:
"Was not Jesus an extremist for love?"

And Abraham Lincoln:
"This nation cannot survive half slave and half free."
And Thomas Jefferson:
"We hold these truths to be self-evident,
that all men are created equal. . . ."

It's not that big of a jump to WCC's Mission Statement.
Among other things, it provides these assurances:
"We provide a caring, open-door
teaching and learning environment.
We provide excellent teaching,
counseling, and support services.
We reach out to people
who have limited income
or other barriers to success.
We enable people to progress
in their academic and career pursuits.
We work in partnership
with the communities we serve."

No doubt the creative extremists
in the English Department
who founded the Writing Center in 1976
knew what was needed
to make good on these assurances.

Let's fast-forward to today.
It has been my great honor and pleasure
to have served as Director of the Writing Center
for 20 years now.

A lot has changed in these past 20 years.
And a whole lot more has changed since 1976.

But the Writing Center's values have not changed.
Our instructors, student tutors, and secretarial staff
—my WCC brothers and sisters—
are committed to sustaining a culture of compassion
and to providing a safe, friendly space
for all members of our community
—students, faculty, staff, alumni, and visitors—
to pursue their dreams and to thrive.

Just as those creative extremists of 1976 did.

In his Letter, King asks:
"Will we be extremists for hate or for love?
Will we be extremists for the preservation of injustice
or for the extension of justice?"

Fellow extremists,
the world needs us,
because we have the necessary answers
to these questions:
Love
And Justice.

Speech delivered at the MLK Day Celebration
Washtenaw Community College
16 Jan 2025

About the Author

Thomas Zimmerman teaches English, directs the Writing Center, and edits *The Big Windows Review* and *The Huron River Review*, at Washtenaw Community College, in Ann Arbor, Michigan, USA. He has received the Distinguished Humanities Educator Award from the Community College Humanities Association and has been nominated for an Association of Community College Trustees Faculty Member Award. Tom has been active in the small press since the 1980s. This is his fifth book with Cyberwit.net, the previous four being *Domestic Sonnets*, *Travel/Travail*, *Dead Man's Quintet*, and *My Night to Cook*.

www.ingramcontent.com/pod-product-compliance
Ingram Content Group UK Ltd.
Pitfield, Milton Keynes, MK11 3LW, UK
UKHW041315190726
13845UKWH00025B/277

9 789363 544758